PRAYERSCRIPTS
Speaking God's Word Book To Him

DISARM THE ENEMY

30 Days of Prayers for

STRIPPING SATAN OF WEAPONS AND INFLUENCE THROUGH THE POWER OF CHRIST

CYRIL OPOKU

Disarm the Enemy: Stripping Satan of Weapons and Influence Through the Power of Christ

Published by *Quest Publications*

ISBN: 978-1-988439-77-8

Cover design by *Quest Publications (questpublications@outlook.com)*

Unless otherwise indicated, all Scripture quotations are taken from the World English Bible WEB, which is in the public domain. For more information, visit: www.worldenglish.bible

This book is a work of devotional encouragement. It is not intended to replace biblical study, pastoral counsel, or professional therapy.

Printed in the United States of America.

First Edition: August 2025

For more books like this, visit *PrayerScripts: https://prayerscripts.org*

Contents

Contents .... *iii*

Preface .... *v*

Introduction .... *vii*

How to Use This Book .... *ix*

Day 1: The Enemy Stripped Bare 1

Day 2: Crushing Satan's Weapons 3

Day 3: Power Over the Enemy 5

Day 4: Resist and Overcome 7

Day 5: Greater is He 8

Day 6: Crush the Enemy's Power 10

Day 7: Armed with Divine Strength 12

Day 8: Kingdoms Brought to Nothing 14

Day 9: Every Knee Must Bow 16

Day 10: Destroyer of Death's Power 17

Day 11: Kept from Falling 19

Day 12: All Under His Feet 21

Day 13: God Upholds My Hand 23

Day 14: Deliverance from Death Traps 25

Day 15: Strangers Submit and Fade 27

Day 16: The Lord Is Faithful 29

Day 17: Through God We Prevail 31

Day 18: Counsel of the Lord Stands 33

Day 19: Frustrate the Devices of Darkness 35

Day 20: End of Affliction Declared 36

Day 21: Strength in My Weakness 37

Day 22: Christ Reigns Over All 39

Day 23: Delivered Into His Kingdom 41

Day 24: By His Spirit Alone 43

Day 25: Victory Is Not in Numbers 44

Day 26: Sword That Disarms 45

Day 27: More Than Conquerors 47

Day 28: If God Is For Us 49

Day 29: He Breaks the Bow 51

Day 30: Love That Never Fails 53

   Epilogue *55*

   Encourage Others with Your Story *57*

   More from PrayerScripts *58*

PREFACE

"No weapon formed against you shall prosper, and every tongue that rises against you in judgment you shall condemn."
—Isaiah 54:17 WEB

The enemy is relentless, and too often, believers are unaware of the subtle ways he attacks. Families are divided, peace is stolen, and destinies are delayed because many Christians have never learned to recognize, confront, and disarm spiritual opposition. This book was written to fill that gap—to equip you with the understanding and tools to take authority over the enemy and reclaim every area of your life and household.

Disarm the Enemy: Stripping Satan of Weapons and Influence Through the Power of Christ was born out of a need for practical, Spirit-led guidance. Too many prayers fail to reach the heart of spiritual attacks because they are generic or reactive. This book is different. It provides Scriptures paired with prophetic, targeted prayers designed to expose and dismantle the schemes of darkness, helping you move from fear and confusion to confidence and victory.

The purpose of this book is to help you walk in awareness, authority, and action. It is meant to awaken your understanding of spiritual warfare, deepen your intimacy with God, and release His power over your life. Every prayer is crafted to strengthen your faith, protect your family, and disarm every weapon the enemy has raised against you.

This is more than a book of prayers—it is a call to spiritual vigilance, a guide to personal empowerment, and a key to living untouchable under the protection of Christ. Step into these pages with faith, boldness, and expectation, knowing that God has provided everything you need to triumph over every scheme of the enemy.

Ready at His command,
Cyril O. *(Illinois, August 2025)*

INTRODUCTION

Have you ever felt the invisible hands of opposition pressing down on your life, your family, or your purpose? Perhaps you've sensed an unseen force trying to steal your peace, disrupt your plans, or sow confusion and fear. This is the reality of the spiritual battlefield—a realm where the enemy seeks to attack, manipulate, and influence every aspect of your life. But there is hope, and that hope is Jesus Christ.

The enemy is real, and his strategies are often subtle, targeting our minds, our homes, and our destinies in ways we may not even notice. To overcome him, we must first recognize his tactics and then respond with authority. This book is designed to do exactly that—to equip you with the spiritual tools and understanding needed to disarm the enemy and reclaim every area of your life.

Inside these pages, you will find Scriptures paired with prophetic, Spirit-led prayers that expose the enemy's schemes and neutralize his influence. Each prayer is carefully crafted to help you confront specific attacks, dismantle strongholds, and enforce God's protection over yourself and your family. They are not generic prayers; they are intentional, precise declarations designed to release the authority you already have in Christ.

You will also discover practical guidance for engaging in spiritual warfare with clarity and confidence. The prayers in this book are organized thematically, so you can address every area of attack— whether it's fear, confusion, division, or oppression. As you move through these pages, you will learn to speak with power, activate God's promises, and walk in victory over every weapon the enemy tries to raise against you.

This is a book of empowerment. It gives you the knowledge, the Scriptures, and the words to take authority over spiritual opposition. With each prayer, expect to see strongholds crumble, peace restored, and God's supernatural protection manifest in your life.

What lies ahead is a journey into spiritual authority, victory, and freedom—an invitation to step boldly into the power Christ has already given you.

How to Use This Book

This is not a book to be rushed through. Each of the 30 prayers is structured as a daily prayer journey, combining the Word of God with prophetic, Spirit-led intercession. Here's how you can make the most of it:

1. **Start with the Scripture** – Each prayer begins with a verse from the World English Bible (WEB). Read it slowly and aloud, letting the Word sink into your heart.

2. **Declare the Word** – Meditate on the key truth in the verse, affirming it as God's unchanging promise.

3. **Pray with Authority** – Use the written prayer as a guide. Speak it boldly, personally, and with conviction. Replace "I" with your name or the names of loved ones as needed.

4. **Journal Insights** – Keep a notebook nearby. Write down any impressions, warnings, or directions you sense from the Holy Spirit.

5. **Build a Rhythm** – Pray one Scripture each day, or linger longer on those that strike you deeply. Repetition builds sharpness, and sharpness builds victory.

Whether you walk through these prayers privately in your devotional time, with your family, or in a small group, the key is consistency. Each prayer is a sword in your hand—use it faithfully.

DAY 1

THE ENEMY STRIPPED BARE

"Having stripped the principalities and the powers, he
made a show of them openly, triumphing over them in it."
— Colossians 2:15 WEB

Almighty Warrior, I exalt You because the cross of Jesus has already
disarmed every principality and power of darkness. I declare boldly
that the enemy holds no weapon that can prevail against me or my
family. The blood of Jesus has broken the chains, stripped the devil
of his authority, and exposed his weakness. He is a defeated foe, and
his arsenal has been emptied.

Father, I stand under the covering of Christ's victory and renounce
every weapon the enemy has tried to wield against my life. I reject
fear, for it has been disarmed. I reject sickness, for it has been
overthrown. I reject every generational curse and demonic
influence, for they have been rendered powerless by the triumph of
the cross.

Lord, let the memory of the enemy's humiliation remind me daily
that I am not fighting for victory but from victory. Let me walk in
confidence, knowing that I am clothed with the full armor of God
and that every fiery dart of the wicked falls to the ground. Father,
strip away the enemy's disguises and show me that his threats are
empty.

I declare over my household that the adversary has no weapons left
that can prosper. Every attempt to re-arm himself against us is

shattered by the Word of the Lord and the power of Christ's blood. Today I walk in boldness, knowing that my enemy has been disarmed, disgraced, and defeated. In Jesus' name, Amen.

DAY 2

CRUSHING SATAN'S WEAPONS

And the God of peace will quickly crush Satan under your
feet. The grace of our Lord Jesus Christ be with you.
— Romans 16:20 WEB

O Lord of Hosts, today I proclaim that Satan's weapons are stripped
and his authority shattered. You are the God of peace, yet You are
also the Warrior who crushes rebellion underfoot. I rise to declare
that every weapon formed against me and my family is nullified by
Your power. No device of darkness shall prevail, no scheme shall
succeed, for You have already promised to crush the adversary
beneath our feet.

Father, I step into the victory purchased at the cross. The enemy's
darts are broken, his snares dismantled, his accusations silenced. I
refuse to fear what the devil plots in the shadows, for Your light
exposes his every plan. Lord, strip him of influence where he seeks
to oppress my mind, my household, my work, and my future.

I declare that the arrows of sickness, fear, confusion, and division
are snapped in two. The sword of deception is taken from his hand.
The chains he designed for my family are broken beyond repair. By
the blood of Jesus, every legal ground he claims is canceled, and
every curse he tries to enforce is void.

God of peace, fill my home with Your presence and surround my
family with Your strength. Let the enemy see that he is powerless,
bound, and defeated. I walk in the authority of Christ, who has

already disarmed principalities and powers. His grace rests upon me, ensuring victory in every battle.

In Jesus' name, Amen.

DAY 3

Power Over the Enemy

"Behold, I give you authority to tread on serpents and scorpions, and over all the power of the enemy. Nothing will in any way hurt you."
—Luke 10:19 WEB

Sovereign Lord, Commander of Heaven's Armies, I stand today in the authority of Jesus Christ, declaring that no weapon formed against me or my family shall prosper. You have given me divine power to trample upon serpents and scorpions, and I will use this authority to expose and disarm every plot of the wicked one.

I decree that the enemy's weapons of fear, sickness, strife, and confusion are rendered useless. Every device of destruction aimed at my household is dismantled by the fire of God. Lord, strip away every tool the enemy has tried to wield against me—whether through words, curses, or secret schemes. His power is broken, and his influence destroyed in the mighty name of Jesus.

Father, I declare that I am untouchable under the covering of the Blood. No arrow that flies by day nor terror that stalks at night will have any effect on me or those connected to me. I trample underfoot every demonic attempt to invade my home, my mind, and my destiny.

Thank You, Lord, that I walk in fearless dominion. By Your Spirit, I am armed with divine authority and clothed with the armor of God.

Today I move forward unshaken, for the enemy has been disarmed, and I reign with Christ in victory.

In Jesus' name, Amen.

DAY 4

Resist and Overcome

Be subject therefore to God. Resist the devil, and he will
flee from you.
— James 4:7 WEB

Almighty Father, today I position myself in humble submission to
You, the Commander of Heaven's armies. Because I am yielded to
You, the power of the enemy is broken. I rise in holy authority,
knowing that as I resist the devil, he must flee—not might flee, but
will flee—because Your Word is unshakable truth.

I disarm every weapon aimed at me and my household. I resist
every lie, every spirit of fear, every whisper of compromise, and
every dark influence. I stand covered under the blood of Jesus, and
no demonic scheme can prosper. My resistance is not in my
strength but in the power of Christ, who lives within me.

Lord, I declare that my home is a fortress of holiness. The enemy
cannot linger here. Every curse spoken, every plot assigned, and
every fiery dart is quenched. As I resist, his grip is broken, and his
weapons are shattered. He cannot stand where God's authority is
enthroned.

I decree that my family and I are hidden in Christ, immune to the
assaults of the wicked one. Submission to You, O God, has secured
our victory. The devil has no choice but to flee in shame and defeat.

In Jesus' name, Amen.

DAY 5

GREATER IS HE

"You are of God, little children, and have overcome them; because greater is he who is in you than he who is in the world."
— 1 John 4:4 WEB

Lord of Hosts, my Mighty Deliverer, I lift my voice in triumph because You dwell within me. Your presence makes me unconquerable, Your Spirit makes me immovable, and Your Word makes me undefeatable. The weapons of the enemy may rise, but they are stripped of power because the Greater One lives in me.

I decree that every demonic weapon fashioned against me and my family is broken. Fear loses its grip, lies lose their influence, and intimidation loses its strength. By the indwelling power of Christ, I disarm every arrow of discouragement, silence every accusation, and nullify every word of witchcraft spoken against us.

The enemy seeks to dominate, but Your Spirit within me releases authority and courage. I will not bow to fear, compromise, or despair. Instead, I rise clothed in Christ, with the assurance that victory is not only possible—it is guaranteed. My family walks in the overflow of this triumph.

Father, let every spiritual weapon in the enemy's arsenal be dismantled by the fire of Your Spirit. Let every demonic plan dissolve into nothingness. I am of God; therefore, I overcome, for the One enthroned within me outshines and overrules the one in the world.

In Jesus' name, Amen.

DAY 6

CRUSH THE ENEMY'S POWER

Through you, will we push down our adversaries. Through
your name, will we tread those who rise up against us.
—Psalm 44:5 WEB

Mighty Warrior and Lord of Hosts, I lift my voice today in the confidence of Your unfailing strength. By Your hand, my enemies are subdued, and by Your power, every adversary that rises against me and my family is trampled underfoot. You are my banner of victory, and in Your name, I advance with holy boldness, knowing no weapon formed against me shall stand.

By the authority of Christ's triumph, I declare that every enemy force set to oppose me is already defeated. Their strategies collapse, their strongholds crumble, and their weapons are stripped away. In Your name, O Lord, I push back the powers of darkness, dismantling every altar of wickedness raised against my household. I tread upon the heads of serpents and scorpions, enforcing the dominion Christ purchased for me with His blood.

Father, I stand clothed in Your armor, shielded by Your Word, and empowered by Your Spirit. Let every enemy scheme be exposed and overturned, and let the shout of victory resound from my life and my family. May the ground beneath my feet testify that the enemy cannot stand where Your name is exalted.

I declare today: the Lord is my victory, my family's victory, and our shield of triumph. The forces of hell are disarmed, and the power of Christ secures my future.

In Jesus' name, Amen.

DAY 7

ARMED WITH DIVINE STRENGTH

For you have armed me with strength to the battle. You
have subdued under me those who rose up against me.
—Psalm 18:39 WEB

O Lord my Strength and Deliverer, I thank You for clothing me with divine might. In the day of battle, I am not left to fight with my own frailty, for You arm me with heavenly power. My adversaries rise, but You subdue them beneath me, stripping them of their courage and silencing their threats. You are the strength of my arm and the shield of my heart.

Father, I step forward as a warrior in Your kingdom, bearing not carnal weapons but the power of Your Spirit and the sharp edge of Your Word. Every enemy spirit, every wicked counsel, every demonic assault is disarmed before me, for the battle belongs to You. I walk forward knowing You have granted me dominion, and You have already decreed the downfall of those who war against my soul and family.

Lord, let Your strength flood my being, granting me stamina to endure, boldness to confront, and authority to conquer. Let the forces of darkness tremble at the sound of Your name spoken through my lips. I declare that no uprising of the enemy shall prevail, for You are my Commander and King.

I proclaim victory, not in my might, but in Yours. My family and I stand covered, equipped, and established in Your strength, and our enemies lie subdued at our feet.

In Jesus' name, Amen.

DAY 8

KINGDOMS BROUGHT TO NOTHING

The seventh angel sounded, and great voices in heaven followed, saying, "The kingdom of the world has become the Kingdom of our Lord and of his Christ. He will reign forever and ever!"
—Revelation 11:15 WEB

Sovereign Lord and Eternal King, I exalt You as the Ruler above all rulers. Every throne, every dominion, every kingdom of this world is swallowed up by the Kingdom of Christ. The kingdoms of darkness that rage against my life and family are brought to nothing, for Your reign is supreme and unshakable.

Father, I declare that the rule of Christ governs my household, my destiny, and my future. No principality can override His authority, and no power of hell can withstand His eternal dominion. The enemy's influence is shattered, his weapons are stripped, and his seat of authority is overturned. I stand under the banner of Christ's everlasting Kingdom, where righteousness, peace, and power prevail.

Lord, let Your Kingdom come in fullness over every area of my life. Let the kingdoms of fear, sickness, lack, and confusion collapse under the weight of Your reign. Replace every shadow of darkness with the blazing light of Your glory. Establish Your throne in my family line, and let the voice of heaven be louder than any voice of opposition.

Today I proclaim: the kingdoms of this world cannot hold me captive. I belong to the unshakable Kingdom of Christ, and in His rule, my enemies are disarmed and silenced forever.

In Jesus' name, Amen.

DAY 9

Every Knee Must Bow

That at the name of Jesus every knee should bow, of those
in heaven, those on earth, and those under the earth.
—Philippians 2:10 WEB

Jesus, Name above all names, I lift high Your authority today. At the
mention of Your name, every force in heaven, on earth, and beneath
the earth must bow. No spirit of darkness can withstand the majesty
of Your Lordship. I invoke Your holy name over my life, my family,
and every battle we face, and I decree: the enemy is disarmed,
bound, and brought to submission.

Father, let every adversary that dares to rise against us be compelled
to bow. Let sickness bend low before You. Let fear and torment
collapse in defeat. Let witchcraft and evil decrees dissolve at the
power of Your name. The sound of "Jesus" shatters strongholds,
breaks chains, and drives out every unclean power that has
attempted to lay claim on our inheritance.

Lord, I exalt You as the unchallenged King. Nothing stands above
You, nothing resists You, and nothing outlasts You. I decree that
every enemy power is beneath my feet because it is already beneath
Yours. The name of Jesus is my weapon, my refuge, and my victory
shout.

So today, I declare over my family: every knee bows, every tongue
confesses, and every enemy is silenced under the rule of Christ. His
name is final authority. In Jesus' name, Amen.

DAY 10

Destroyer of Death's Power

Since then the children have shared in flesh and blood, he
also himself in the same way partook of the same, that
through death he might bring to nothing him who had the
power of death, that is, the devil.
—Hebrews 2:14 WEB

Lord Jesus, my Victor and Redeemer, I glorify You for partaking of
flesh and blood, for stepping into the battlefield of humanity.
Through Your death, You shattered the dominion of the one who
held the power of death. The devil is stripped, disarmed, and
brought to nothing. His grip over my life and family is broken
forever.

I declare that death has no victory over me, for You conquered the
grave. The terror of the enemy has been dismantled, and his threats
lie powerless at my feet. My household is covered by the blood of
Jesus, the blood that proclaims eternal life, healing, and
deliverance. The voice of death and destruction is silenced by the
voice of the risen Christ.

Father, I decree that every demonic agenda to cut short destinies,
to steal life, or to bring generational destruction is nullified. The
enemy cannot hold sway over our years, our health, or our future.
Because Christ has conquered, we live under the banner of life
abundant and life eternal.

So I rise in bold confidence, declaring: the devil is defeated, death is swallowed in victory, and my family walks in the triumph of the cross. Christ's death has disarmed the destroyer, and His resurrection secures our everlasting freedom.

In Jesus' name, Amen.

DAY 11

KEPT FROM FALLING

"Now to him who is able to keep them from stumbling, and to present you faultless before the presence of his glory in great joy."
— Jude 1:24 WEB

Almighty Keeper of my soul, I lift my voice in triumph because You alone have the power to sustain me and my household. You do not allow our feet to slip into snares laid by the enemy. You hold us steady when the adversary plots our downfall, and You present us blameless before Your glory with joy. I declare that every scheme of darkness is already disarmed by the power of Your keeping hand.

Lord, I stand in the assurance that no trap of sin, no deception, and no hidden weapon of the enemy can prevail against me or my family. You have stripped the enemy of his accusations, silencing his claims, and rendering powerless every spirit that seeks to condemn. My destiny is preserved by Your covenant faithfulness, and my future is anchored in the joy of Your presence.

Father, where the adversary attempts to weaken our walk, strengthen our footing. Where he tries to entice with stumbling blocks, lift us up in Your mercy. I declare that my life and the lives of my loved ones are secured on the Rock of Ages. No weapon of shame, no snare of guilt, no arrow of reproach will cause us to fall.

By the power of the blood of Jesus, I decree stability, holiness, and victory over every force that conspires against us. I walk upright in

Your truth and rejoice that the grip of the enemy has been broken. My steps are ordered by the Lord, and we are presented faultless in Your sight.

In Jesus' name, Amen.

DAY 12

ALL UNDER HIS FEET

"He put all things in subjection under his feet, and gave
him to be head over all things for the assembly."
— Ephesians 1:22 WEB

King of Kings and Ruler of all creation, I exalt You because every
power, principality, and dominion is already under the feet of
Christ. Nothing in heaven, on earth, or beneath the earth can rival
His authority. And because I belong to You, I share in the victory
that You have secured. My enemies have already been disarmed,
their weapons shattered by the supremacy of Your Son.

Lord, I declare that every spirit of oppression, every voice of
accusation, and every device of wickedness aimed at me or my
household is beneath the authority of Jesus. The headship of Christ
over His Church means that we are covered, defended, and upheld
by His mighty reign. I rest in the assurance that no adversary can
rise above the name of Jesus or undo the triumph of the cross.

Father, I decree that my life and my family's lives are aligned under
the headship of Christ. Every power that attempts to manipulate,
intimidate, or dominate us must bow. Every altar raised against us
crumbles under the weight of His dominion. We are hidden in
Christ, and our authority is rooted in His finished work.

Therefore, I speak peace, protection, and victory over our home. I
stand boldly in the truth that Christ reigns, and I tread upon the
works of darkness with holy confidence. Nothing can withstand the

rule of my Savior. All things are under His feet, and we are safe in His covering.

In Jesus' name, Amen.

DAY 13

GOD UPHOLDS MY HAND

"For I, Yahweh your God, will hold your right hand, saying to you, 'Don't be afraid. I will help you.'"
— Isaiah 41:13 WEB

Faithful Deliverer, I lift my hands in surrender and thanksgiving, for You have promised to uphold me with Your own mighty hand. I do not face the battles of life alone. You grip my right hand with strength, steadying me against every attack of the enemy. You whisper courage to my spirit and strip fear from my heart.

Lord, I declare that my adversaries are already disarmed, for Your help surrounds me like a shield. No terror of the night, no arrow by day, and no voice of intimidation will prevail over me or my family. You, O God, are my helper. You shatter the weapons of those who rise against me, and You silence the tongue of those who mock and accuse.

Father, I decree that as You hold my hand, You also hold the hand of my children, my spouse, and all those under my covering. We are preserved by Your strength, and the grip of the enemy is broken. Where he tries to sow fear, You sow peace. Where he seeks to weaken, You empower. Where he tries to scatter, You gather us in safety.

Therefore, I walk in boldness, knowing that the Almighty One is my constant help. I will not fear demonic plots, ancestral curses, or generational chains, for the hand of the Lord is with me. I move forward in courage, advancing in destiny, and rejoicing in my deliverance.

In Jesus' name, Amen.

DAY 14

Deliverance from Death Traps

"To hear the groaning of the prisoner; to free those who
are condemned to death."
— Psalm 102:20 WEB

God of Mercy and Deliverance, I cry out in victory because You
bend Your ear to the cries of the afflicted. You do not ignore the
groaning of those bound in chains, but You rise to set captives free.
Every death sentence spoken over me or my household is reversed
by the blood of Jesus. Every snare of destruction prepared by the
enemy is exposed and destroyed.

Lord, I proclaim that my family and I will not be bound by spiritual
prisons. The shackles of fear, infirmity, addiction, and oppression
are broken in Your presence. You redeem us from pits of despair
and cancel every decree of death that the enemy has inscribed. I
declare that life, freedom, and restoration are our inheritance.

Father, where the enemy has sought to silence my voice, You
empower my song. Where he has sought to enslave with guilt,
shame, or torment, You release liberty. Every demonic jailer is
stripped of authority, and every chain forged against us melts before
the fire of Your Spirit.

I stand in holy boldness and decree that my house is free. We are
lifted from dungeons of fear into the glorious light of Your
salvation. No prison door can resist Your command. No judgment

of death can withstand the voice of Your covenant. We walk out in liberty, and the enemy's devices are left in ruins.

In Jesus' name, Amen.

DAY 15

STRANGERS SUBMIT AND FADE

"As soon as they hear of me they shall obey me. The foreigners shall submit themselves to me."
— Psalm 18:44 WEB

Mighty Conqueror, I lift my voice in praise because You cause the nations and strangers to bow at the sound of Your name. Those who once rose against me in arrogance are subdued by the authority of Christ in me. Every foreign spirit, every intruder of darkness, every uninvited power trespassing in my life or family is forced into submission.

Lord, I declare that demonic strangers lose their hold over my destiny. They cannot resist the command of the Lord nor defy the covenant sealed by the blood of Jesus. At the sound of the Word, they bow and flee. At the mention of Your name, they surrender their influence. The weapons of intimidation and oppression crumble in their hands.

Father, I decree that my household is no dwelling place for strangers. Every power that crept in through ancestral gates, covenants, or hidden agreements is cast out. Foreign spirits of fear, infirmity, strife, or poverty are disarmed and expelled. My territory is cleansed, and my inheritance is restored.

I rise in the authority of Christ and declare dominion over my sphere. The strangers of darkness hear the command of the Lord and submit without resistance. I walk in authority, clothed in victory, rejoicing that You, O God, have made my enemies bow before me.

In Jesus' name, Amen.

DAY 16

THE LORD IS FAITHFUL

But the Lord is faithful, who will establish you, and guard
you from the evil one.
—2 Thessalonians 3:3 WEB

Mighty Father, Faithful and True, I lift my heart before You in full
confidence that You are my Keeper and the Shield of my life. You
are not a man that You should lie, nor the son of man that You
should change Your mind. Your faithfulness stands unshaken
through every generation, and today I declare that no weapon
formed against me or my family will stand, because the Lord
Himself establishes us and guards us from the evil one.

I proclaim that the hands of the adversary are broken over my
destiny. Every weapon fashioned in the secret places of darkness is
dismantled, and every scheme designed against my household is
disarmed. Lord, You surround me with Your power and clothe me
with Your righteousness. By the authority of Your Word, I decree
that we are planted firmly in Your will, immovable and
untouchable, defended by the blood of the Lamb.

O Covenant-keeping God, strip the enemy of his influence over my
mind, my health, my marriage, my children, and my future. Where
he seeks to sow confusion, release Your divine order. Where he
attempts to establish fear, breathe the strength of Your Spirit into
me. Where he tries to plant discouragement, let the joy of the Lord
break forth like light at dawn.

Faithful Guardian, I rest secure under Your watch. I reject every lie of the enemy and stand established in Your unfailing truth. I shall not be moved, for You are the wall of fire around me and the glory within me. Your faithfulness is my fortress and my defense.

In Jesus' name, Amen.

DAY 17

Through God We Prevail

Through God we will do valiantly, for it is he who will tread down our adversaries.
—Psalm 60:12 WEB

Warrior King, I lift my voice in triumph because my victory is not in my own strength but in Yours. You are the Lord of Hosts, the Captain of the armies of heaven, and it is by Your might that I overcome. I declare boldly that every adversary rising against me and my household shall be trampled underfoot, for the Lord Himself goes before me as a consuming fire.

Father, I renounce the power of fear, defeat, and oppression. I declare that through You, I fight valiantly, I speak courageously, and I stand victoriously. My enemies are powerless before the thunder of Your presence. Every spirit of infirmity, bondage, and delay is crushed under the feet of my Redeemer. Every adversary of my progress is stripped of strength and rendered helpless before the light of Your glory.

Lord, clothe me in Your armor. Strengthen my hands for battle and my heart with boldness. Let every valley of discouragement be lifted and every mountain of resistance crumble. Cause my life to resound with the testimony that my God treads down my enemies and establishes my steps on high places.

Today, I proclaim that the victories of my family are permanent and sealed by Your Word. We march forward in courage, advancing under Your banner. We will not retreat, for You, O Lord, are our Victory and Deliverer.

In Jesus' name, Amen.

DAY 18

COUNSEL OF THE LORD STANDS

Yahweh brings the counsel of the nations to nothing. He
makes the thoughts of the peoples to be of no effect. The
counsel of Yahweh stands fast forever, the thoughts of his
heart to all generations.
—Psalm 33:10-11 WEB

Eternal Father, I magnify You as the Sovereign One whose counsel
cannot be overturned. Kings may gather, nations may scheme, and
adversaries may conspire, but every plan opposed to You dissolves
into dust. Today, I declare that every counsel of darkness against me
and my family is nullified, shattered, and made powerless.

O God of wisdom, silence the voice of the accuser, strip the enemy
of influence, and scatter the plots spoken in hidden places. Let the
whispers of witchcraft fall mute. Let the decrees of evil councils
collapse like walls of Jericho. You alone speak, and it is established.
Your counsel stands firm from everlasting to everlasting.

Lord, anchor my life in Your thoughts and establish my family in
Your will. No generational curse, no demonic device, and no
ungodly alliance can undo the word You have spoken over us. Let
Your divine plan prevail, and let Your kingdom purposes be
revealed in our lives. We submit ourselves to Your perfect counsel
that guides, protects, and prospers.

I decree that the destiny of my household is secured in Christ,
immune to satanic interference, preserved by the unchanging

Word of God. Nations may rage, but the counsel of the Lord concerning me and my children will stand unbroken.

In Jesus' name, Amen.

DAY 19

FRUSTRATE THE DEVICES OF DARKNESS

He frustrates the devices of the crafty, so that their hands
can't perform their enterprise.
—Job 5:12 WEB

Almighty God, You are the great Disruptor of the enemy's schemes.
You sit enthroned above all powers, and You frustrate the plots of
the wicked until their hands are rendered useless. Today, I declare
that every device of darkness against my life and my household is
dismantled, scattered, and void of effect.

Father, let every evil project raised against us collapse under the
weight of Your judgment. Cause the hands that reach for my destiny
to wither, and the tools of oppression to fail. I decree that demonic
traps, snares of deception, and weapons of manipulation are
shattered by the authority of Jesus' blood.

Lord, where the enemy has crafted webs of confusion, untangle
them by the fire of Your Spirit. Where evil hands are stretched to
seize opportunity, cut them off. Where tongues have been
sharpened to slander and accuse, silence them with Your truth.
Every agenda of the wicked is overturned, and every weapon
formed against us shall not prosper.

I stand in the covenant of protection, declaring that the plans of
darkness are exposed and frustrated. My family walks in the victory
of Christ, preserved from every attack, and hidden under the
shadow of the Almighty. In Jesus' name, Amen.

DAY 20

END OF AFFLICTION DECLARED

He will make a full end. Affliction won't rise up the second time.
—Nahum 1:9 WEB

Lord of Hosts, I lift my heart in thanksgiving, for You are the God who brings finality to the battles of life. You do not allow affliction to have the last word. Today, I stand in Your promise that every torment of the enemy, every cycle of bondage, and every repeated attack is brought to an end by Your decree.

I declare that the yoke of oppression is broken, and the rod of the enemy is shattered. The sicknesses that linger, the troubles that repeat, and the torments that resurface are commanded to cease forever. By the blood of Jesus, I draw a line that the adversary cannot cross. My household is delivered, our inheritance is secure, and our peace is unshakable.

Father, silence every voice that calls for a second wave of destruction. Shut the mouth of the accuser, and close the door to generational affliction. Let the fire of Your Spirit burn up every cycle of defeat, and let the oil of Your covenant flow over us, bringing rest and restoration.

Today, I prophesy a new season over my life and family—cycles of pain are broken, and cycles of blessing are established. What once plagued us will not rise again. The Lord has spoken a full end, and it is done. In Jesus' name, Amen.

DAY 21

STRENGTH IN MY WEAKNESS

My flesh and my heart fails, but God is the strength of my
heart and my portion forever.
—Psalm 73:26 WEB

O Lord, my Rock and my Redeemer, I come before You with
gratitude that You are the unshakable strength of my heart. When
my own flesh falters, when my strength proves too fragile for the
battles I face, You arise as my everlasting portion. I declare today
that my enemies cannot prevail against me or my household, for
You sustain me beyond the weakness of mortal strength.

Father, I prophetically decree that every weapon of
discouragement, sickness, or despair the enemy has raised against
me is disarmed. My body may tire, my emotions may waver, but
You, the Living God, empower me with unfailing might. I strip the
adversary of his influence over my mind and family, declaring that
his lies and accusations will not hold dominion, for the Lord
Himself is our strength.

Holy One, in You I rise above natural limitations. I speak over my
life and family that the power of the enemy is nullified, and the
sufficiency of Christ carries us forward. Where weakness once
ruled, divine power now reigns. I choose to stand in covenant
strength, knowing that our portion is eternal and cannot be stolen.

So I lift my voice in faith: we are upheld, sustained, and made
unassailable in the strength of our God. No enemy can prevail

against us because we stand clothed in the strength of the Almighty. In Jesus' name, Amen.

DAY 22

CHRIST REIGNS OVER ALL

For he must reign until he has put all his enemies under his feet. The last enemy that will be abolished is death. For, "He put all things in subjection under his feet." But when he says, "All things are put in subjection," it is evident that he is excepted who subjected all things to him.
—1 Corinthians 15:25-27 WEB

King of Glory, I exalt You as the One whose reign has no end. You have subdued every enemy under Your feet, and I align myself under the victory of Christ Jesus. I prophetically declare that no power of darkness, no curse, no generational bondage, and no scheme of Satan has authority over me or my family. We are hidden in the One who reigns until every foe is fully abolished.

Lord Jesus, I decree that the weapons of death, destruction, and despair are disarmed from my household. You are the Resurrection and the Life, and by Your dominion, every plan of the enemy crumbles. I invoke the authority of Your victory, declaring that my life, my bloodline, and my destiny are under the rule of Christ, not the manipulation of darkness.

Father, I step into the assurance that Christ's reign covers every area of my life. My family is seated with Him in heavenly places, far above principalities and powers. Every voice of opposition is silenced, every adversary is stripped of influence, and the shadow of death holds no sway over us.

Today I confess boldly: the reign of Christ rules over my household. We live under His dominion, and His enemies are our defeated foes. Therefore, we walk in triumph, unshaken and victorious. In Jesus' name, Amen.

DAY 23

DELIVERED INTO HIS KINGDOM

who delivered us out of the power of darkness, and
translated us into the Kingdom of the Son of his love, in
whom we have our redemption, the forgiveness of our
sins.
—Colossians 1:13-14 WEB

Father of Lights, I praise You for the mighty deliverance wrought
through the blood of Jesus. You have snatched me and my family
out of the grip of darkness and translated us into the glorious
Kingdom of Your beloved Son. I declare that no chain of bondage,
no weapon of oppression, and no power of the enemy can drag us
back into captivity.

By the power of redemption, I disarm the strategies of the wicked
one against my household. Every plot of darkness is overturned,
and every demonic assignment is canceled. Our sins are forgiven,
and our lives are covered by the blood of Jesus; therefore, the
accuser has no legal ground to stand against us.

O Redeemer, I declare prophetically that we are citizens of a higher
Kingdom where righteousness, peace, and joy in the Holy Spirit
reign. The dominion of darkness has been stripped from our lives,
our health, our finances, and our destinies. We live under the
covering of divine light, and the works of the enemy are shattered.

So I stand today in triumph, proclaiming that we are delivered and
secured in Christ's Kingdom. Our inheritance cannot be stolen, our

future cannot be sabotaged, and our redemption is eternal. In Jesus' name, Amen.

DAY 24

BY HIS SPIRIT ALONE

Then he answered and spoke to me, saying, "This is
Yahweh's word to Zerubbabel, saying, 'Not by might, nor
by power, but by my Spirit,' says Yahweh of Armies.
—Zechariah 4:6 WEB

Almighty God, Commander of Heaven's armies, I lift my voice in
surrender to Your Spirit. I acknowledge that my human strength
cannot conquer the adversary, nor can fleshly might deliver me
from the grip of darkness. But by Your Spirit, O Lord, the enemy is
disarmed, and the weapons raised against my family are broken.

I decree prophetically that the Spirit of the Living God rises as a
shield around my household. Every fortress of wickedness is pulled
down, not by my own ability, but by the breath of God. I strip the
enemy of influence over my life, declaring that no earthly might can
compare with the Spirit who broods over me with power.

Father, let Your Spirit flood every corner of my existence—my
mind, my home, my relationships. By Your Spirit, confusion is
scattered, fear is destroyed, and every satanic scheme is nullified.
The adversary may have trusted in power and deception, but I stand
in the might of the Spirit of Yahweh.

Therefore, I rise today as a warrior empowered by the Holy Ghost.
Not by human effort, not by earthly strategies, but by the Spirit of
God, the enemy is rendered powerless, and my family stands
untouchable. In Jesus' name, Amen.

DAY 25

VICTORY IS NOT IN NUMBERS

There is no king saved by the multitude of an army. A
mighty man is not delivered by great strength.
—Psalm 33:16 WEB

Sovereign Lord, I magnify You as the One who rules above armies
and powers. The salvation of my family does not depend on the
strength of men or the numbers of those who stand with us. You
alone are our deliverer, and I put my trust not in the arm of flesh
but in the arm of the Almighty.

I prophetically declare that the strategies of the enemy are
disarmed, for they rely on human strength, deception, and
numbers, but I rely on the Lord of Hosts. No multitude of
adversaries can overcome the covenant-keeping God who fights for
me and my household. The enemy's strength is broken, and his
influence is shattered because the Lord is our refuge.

Father, I decree that every alliance, every confederacy of
wickedness, and every network of darkness raised against my life
collapses. Their numbers do not intimidate me, for You, Lord, are
greater than the host of the wicked. I choose to trust in Your saving
power that cannot be measured by human standards.

So I rise today in unshakable confidence: my victory is not by
numbers, not by strength, but by the saving hand of Yahweh. My
household is secured, and the weapons of the enemy are stripped
of power. In Jesus' name, Amen.

DAY 26

Sword That Disarms

Take the helmet of salvation, and the sword of the Spirit,
which is the word of God.
—Ephesians 6:17 WEB

O Mighty God, I lift my voice as a warrior armed by Your Spirit.
You have not left me vulnerable, but You have placed in my hand
the sword of Your Word and on my head the covering of salvation.
I declare that every scheme of the enemy against me and my family
is disarmed, for no weapon formed against us can endure the power
of Your Spirit.

Lord of Hosts, let the living Word in my mouth pierce through the
strategies of darkness. Where the enemy whispers lies, I cut them
down with truth. Where he brings fear, I strike with the confidence
of salvation. Where he tries to entangle me with temptation, I sever
the cords with the sharp edge of Your promises. I am not
defenseless, for I stand clothed in the armor of Christ.

Father, I release Your Word into the atmosphere of my home, into
the hearts of my children, and over every pursuit of my family. Let
it build a wall of fire the enemy cannot breach. Let it scatter the
adversary's camp and silence the arrows of accusation hurled
against us.

Today I wield this sword with authority. By Your Spirit, I dismantle
strongholds, uproot wicked foundations, and cancel every hidden
plot. The enemy is stripped of influence, because Your salvation is

my crown and Your Word is my weapon. Victory is ours, for I stand under the banner of Christ, mighty in battle.

In Jesus' name, Amen.

DAY 27

More Than Conquerors

No, in all these things, we are more than conquerors
through him who loved us.
—Romans 8:37 WEB

Faithful Father, I rise today under the covering of Your unfailing love. You declare me not only a conqueror but more than a conqueror through Christ Jesus. I refuse to cower beneath the lies of the enemy or bow to the threats of darkness, because the love of Christ makes me unshakable.

Lord of Glory, every battle the enemy wages against my mind, my health, my family, and my destiny is already overturned by Your victory at the cross. His weapons fall powerless, his accusations collapse, and his intimidation scatters like chaff before the wind. Your love has wrapped me in triumph that cannot be undone.

I speak over my household today: we are not victims, we are victors. We are not oppressed, we are upheld by the everlasting arms of God. No curse, no fear, no spiritual attack can reduce us, because the power that raised Christ from the grave lives in us. Your love is the shield that preserves our lives and the sword that crushes our adversary.

Almighty God, I stand firm and fearless. By the blood of Jesus, I declare that every chain of bondage is broken, every snare of deception is shattered, and every enemy influence is disarmed. I walk boldly into my inheritance as one crowned with victory, carrying the banner of Christ's love into every battle.

In Jesus' name, Amen.

DAY 28

If God Is For Us

What then shall we say about these things? If God is for
us, who can be against us?
—Romans 8:31 WEB

O Sovereign Lord, I bow before You with awe and thanksgiving, for
Your presence on my side is the assurance of unstoppable victory.
If You are for me, then every adversary is already defeated, every
scheme of darkness already undone. Your word silences every fear,
for no one can stand against the power of the Almighty.

Mighty Defender, I disarm every voice of accusation that rises
against me and my family. I nullify every curse, hex, or hidden plot
of the enemy, because none can prosper when You are my Shield
and my Fortress. The enemy may rise, but he will fall before the
greatness of my God.

Today, I anchor myself in this truth: no opposition can overthrow
Your will for my life. No demonic force, no earthly adversary, no
spiritual darkness has permission to prevail against the covenant
sealed by the blood of Jesus. I rest under the unshakable covering
of Your divine favor.

Father, I release this word into the atmosphere of my destiny: we
are untouchable under Your hand. Every plan of sabotage is
scattered. Every weapon forged against my children is broken.
Every chain of fear is consumed by Your fire. I march forward

knowing that You, the Almighty, are with me and my household, and therefore we cannot be defeated.

In Jesus' name, Amen.

DAY 29

HE BREAKS THE BOW

He makes wars cease to the end of the earth. He breaks the
bow, and cuts the spear in two. He burns the chariots in
the fire.
—Psalm 46:9 WEB

O Lord of Hosts, my Warrior and Deliverer, I lift my hands to the
One who breaks the power of the enemy. You are the God who
shatters the bow, who destroys the spear, who sets fire to the
chariots of war. I declare today that every weapon raised against me
and my family is broken by the hand of the Almighty.

Holy Father, silence the wars stirred up against our minds, our
health, and our destiny. Where the enemy has drawn his bow to
launch arrows of sickness, fear, or confusion, break it in two. Where
he has lifted his spear to strike with affliction, cut it down. Where
he has prepared chariots of destruction, consume them with Your
holy fire.

I decree peace over my household—the peace that comes from You
alone, not as the world gives. Let the ceaseless warfare against our
advancement, our marriages, our children, and our future be
stopped by Your divine command. Cause the battles that raged in
the spirit to be overturned in the courts of heaven.

God of Power, disarm every enemy force and dismantle every
satanic weapon. Cover us under the refuge of Your presence, where

no evil can penetrate. Today I stand victorious, for the Lord of Hosts has entered the battlefield and secured my peace.

In Jesus' name, Amen.

DAY 30

LOVE THAT NEVER FAILS

Nor height, nor depth, nor any other created thing will be able to separate us from God's love, which is in Christ Jesus our Lord.
—Romans 8:39 WEB

Everlasting Father, I exalt You for the unfailing power of Your love. Nothing in all creation—no power of hell, no scheme of man, no depth of darkness—can ever separate me or my family from the love that is in Christ Jesus. Your love is my fortress and the disarming force against the enemy's attacks.

O God of steadfast mercy, I declare that the grip of fear is broken, the chains of condemnation are shattered, and the voice of the accuser is silenced. The enemy seeks to separate me from Your presence, but Your love surrounds me like a shield, refusing to let me go. He has no weapon strong enough to sever the covenant sealed in Christ's blood.

I decree over my household that we are anchored in unshakable love. No curse can override it, no spirit of rejection can undo it, and no darkness can extinguish it. The love of Christ disarms every assault of hatred, envy, strife, and division. We stand secure in the embrace of the Almighty.

Father, let this love rise as a blazing fire around my home. Let it consume bitterness, drive out fear, and fortify us against the attacks of the enemy. With this love as our shield, we walk in victory, unbreakable, unstoppable, untouchable.

In Jesus' name, Amen.

EPILOGUE

The battles you have faced, the prayers you have prayed, and the truths you have claimed in these pages are only the beginning. Spiritual warfare is not a one-time event—it is a lifestyle of awareness, authority, and action. Now that you have armed yourself with Scripture, prophetic prayers, and the knowledge of your authority in Christ, the question remains: what will you do next?

The challenge is to move from reading and praying to living victoriously every day. The enemy will continue to scheme, but you are no longer defenseless. Take what you have learned here and apply it relentlessly. Speak the Word aloud, declare God's promises over your family, and identify areas where opposition still seeks to operate. Let these prayers become your weaponry, your shield, and your daily declaration of victory.

This is your call to spiritual vigilance. Do not allow the enemy to regain ground that has been reclaimed in Christ. Continue to grow in discernment, deepen your intimacy with God, and take authority boldly. Every victory you experience is a testimony of God's power, a demonstration of His faithfulness, and a step toward the full manifestation of His plans for your life.

Remember, the spiritual life is active, not passive. The prayers in this book are your starting point, but now it is time to stand firm, advance with confidence, and enforce the protection and favor of

God over every sphere of your existence. The battle continues, but so does your authority.

Step forward, be vigilant, and let victory become your lifestyle. The enemy has been disarmed, but your journey of triumph in Christ is only beginning.

Encourage Others with Your Story

If this prayer guide has strengthened your faith, deepened your intercession, or helped you stand in the gap, would you consider leaving a short review on Amazon? Your feedback not only encourages others but also helps more believers discover this resource and join in the prayer movement. Every review—just a few sentences—makes a difference. Thank you for being part of this movement.

MORE FROM PRAYERSCRIPTS

COMMAND YOUR DESTINY SERIES

Command Your Morning:

30 Days of Prayers and Declarations to Seize Your Day and Shape Your Destiny

There is a battle over every morning—and every believer must choose to either drift into the day or command it.

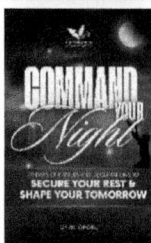

Command Your Night:

30 Days of Prayers and Declarations to Secure Your Rest and Shape Your Tomorrow

Every night is a spiritual battlefield—what you do before you sleep can determine the course of your tomorrow.

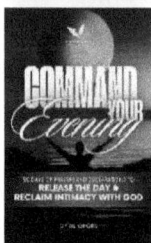

Command Your Evening:

30 Days of Prayers and Declarations to Release the Day and Reclaim Intimacy with God

There is a battle over every transition—and evening is one of the most spiritually neglected.

EXPOSING THE ENEMY SERIES

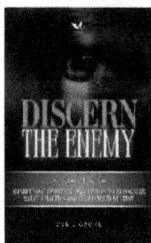

Discern the Enemy:

Sharpening Spiritual Perception to Recognize Satan's Tactics and Guard Your Destiny

The greatest danger is not the enemy you can see—it is the one you cannot. Can you recognize the enemy before he strikes?

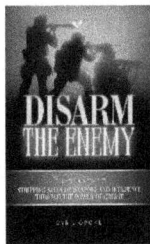

Disarm the Enemy:

Stripping Satan of Weapons and Influence Through the Power of Christ

Are you tired of feeling like the enemy has the upper hand in your life? It's time to take back your ground, silence the lies of darkness, and walk in the unstoppable authority of Christ.

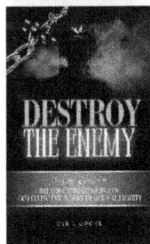

Destroy the Enemy:

Breaking Strongholds and Cancelling Evil Works by God's Authority

Are you tired of living under the weight of unseen battles? It's time to rise up and destroy the enemy's works in your life.

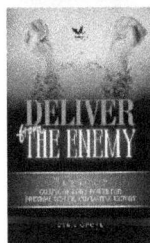

Deliver from the Enemy:

Calling on God's Power for Freedom, Rescue, and Lasting Victory

Break free from spiritual attacks and experience God's mighty deliverance in every battle.

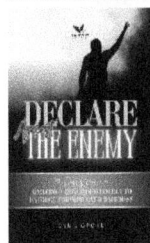

Declare Against the Enemy:

Speaking God's Word Boldly to Enforce Triumph Over Darkness

What if you could silence the enemy's schemes, protect your family, and walk boldly into every God-ordained assignment with unshakable authority?

SPIRITUAL WARFARE SERIES

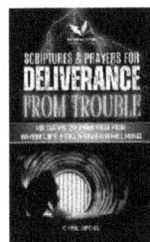

Scriptures & Prayers for Deliverance from Trouble:

40 Days of Prayer for When Life Feels Overwhelming

Are you walking through a season where life feels heavy and your prayers feel weak?

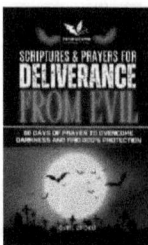

Scriptures & Prayers for Deliverance from Evil:

50 Days of Prayer to Overcome Darkness and Find God's Protection

When darkness presses in, how do you pray?

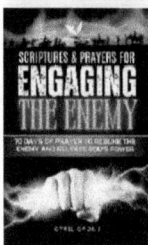

Scriptures & Prayers for Engaging the Enemy:

70 Days of Prayer to Rebuke the Enemy and Release God's Power

You weren't called to run from the battle—you were anointed to win it.

Scriptures & Prayers for Combating Spiritual Wickedness:

50 Days of Prayer to Overthrow Wicked Plans and Stand in God's Victory

Are you facing opposition that feels deeper than the natural? You're not imagining it—and you're not powerless.

THE BLOOD COVENANT SERIES

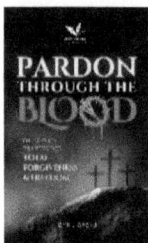

Pardon Through the Blood:

60 Days of Prayers for Total Forgiveness and Freedom

Guilt is a prison. The blood of Jesus holds the key.

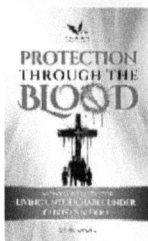

Protection Through the Blood:

60 Days of Prayers for Living Untouchable Under Christ's Blood

You are not helpless. You are not exposed. You are covered—completely—by the blood of Jesus.

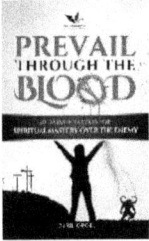

Prevail Through the Blood:

60 Days of Prayers for Spiritual Mastery Over the Enemy

What if every scheme of the enemy against your life could be dismantled—by one unstoppable weapon?

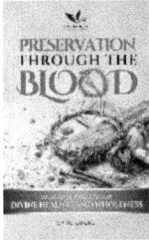

Preservation Through the Blood:

60 Days of Prayers for Divine Healing and Wholeness

Unlock Lasting Healing and Wholeness Through the Blood of Jesus

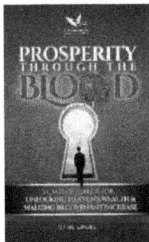

Prosperity Through the Blood:

60 Days of Prayers for Unlocking Heaven's Wealth and Walking in Covenant Increase

You were redeemed for more than survival—you were redeemed to prosper.

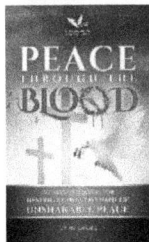

Peace Through the Blood:

60 Days of Prayers for Resting in the Covenant of Unshakable Peace

Are you ready to silence every storm of the mind, heart, and home—once and for all?

Standing in the Gap for Covenant Awakening:

30 Days of Prayer for National Repentance, Righteous Leadership & God's Sovereign Rule

What if your prayers could help turn the tide of a nation?

Standing in the Gap for Divine Defense:

30 Days of Prayer for National Guidance, Guarding & Glory

When the foundations of a nation feel as if they're shaking, prayer is the strongest fortress you can build.

Standing in the Gap for National Healing:

40 Days of Prayer for Reconciliation, Righteousness, and Restoration

What if your prayers could help heal a nation? What if God is waiting for someone—like you—to stand in the gap?

Standing in the Gap for The President:

50 Days of Prayer for Leadership, Loyalty, and Lifeline

When a nation's leader is under spiritual siege, will you answer the call to stand in the gap?

www.ingramcontent.com/pod-product-compliance
Lightning Source LLC
Chambersburg PA
CBHW060157070426
42447CB00033B/2194